PRESENTED TO:

FROM:

DATE:

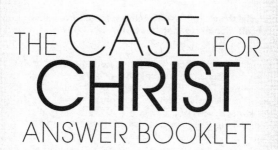

THE CASE FOR CHRIST
ANSWER BOOKLET

LEE STROBEL

ZONDERVAN®

ZONDERVAN

The Case for Christ Answer Booklet

Copyright © 2017 by Lee Strobel

Requests for information should be addressed to:

Zondervan, 3900 Sparks Dr. SE, Grand Rapids, Michigan 49546

Special thanks to Mark Mittelberg for his invaluable contribution to creating this booklet.

ISBN 978-0-310-08982-7

Printed in the United States of America

20 21   LSC   10 9 8 7 6

Contents

Introduction ix

1. I have so many questions—and a few
   doubts—about the Christian faith.
   What should I do with them? 1

2. Were there really ancient prophecies
   predicting details about the life and
   ministry of Jesus? 3

3. Is there any historical evidence from
   outside the Bible to show it is true? 7

4. With all the differences between the
   New Testament manuscripts, how
   can we trust the Bible? 9

5. Was Jesus really convinced he was
   the Son of God? 11

6. Jesus called himself the "Son of Man."
   Doesn't this mean he was merely
   human? 13

7. Did Jesus' life demonstrate that he
   was a divine person? 15

8. Jesus did many things, but what was
   his real mission? 17

9. The New Testament says Jesus sweat drops of blood when he was praying in the Garden of Gethsemane. Is that just a figure of speech? 19

10. A central claim of Christianity is that Jesus rose from the dead. Is there any solid evidence to support this? 21

11. Some people claim Jesus' tomb was empty because someone stole his body. How do we know that's not what happened? 25

12. Jesus appeared to his followers after his crucifixion—but how do we know they weren't just hallucinating? 27

13. Weren't the reports of Jesus' death and resurrection written generations later—possibly distorting the story? . . . 29

14. What difference does it make today that a man rose from the dead two thousand years ago? 31

15. How can belief in the resurrection of Christ impact someone personally? . . 33

16. Isn't it narrow-minded to claim that Jesus is the only pathway to God? 35

17. There are so many other religions out there. How can we be sure that Christianity is the right one? 37

18. You've said you came to realize you didn't have enough faith to maintain your atheism. Can you explain what you mean? 39

19. Now that we've explored a lot of questions and answers, what should I do with the information? 42

20. Honestly, this is all starting to make sense. But how can I know for sure that my sins are forgiven and I'm part of God's family? 44

Notes 47

Recommended Resources 50

Meet Lee Strobel 53

Introduction

As portrayed in *The Case for Christ* book and movie, the questions discussed in this booklet once represented huge barriers in my quest for the truth about the identity of Christ, his mission and miracles, and his alleged resurrection.

> Why do people believe God exists at all? How can we know Jesus was the Son of God? Can we really trust the New Testament as reliable history? Can a thinking person accept the idea of a man rising from the dead? Is there evidence for any of these things? And even if it's all true, what difference does it make for my life today?

For a season, these questions haunted me. But gradually, after lots of research, deep discussions, and extended times of reflection, the answers I found began to assure me that the case for Christianity was strong. Maybe there is a God. And maybe Jesus really is God's Son who came to live, die, and return from the grave—all on our behalf.

Increasingly *The Case for Christ* became convincing to me. After nearly two years of searching, I opened myself up to the truth that there is a heavenly Father, that Jesus is the Savior, and that he had been gently pursuing me all along. Finally, I humbled myself and prayed to receive Christ as my forgiver and leader.

It was a decision I've never regretted—and one I'm confident you'll be glad you've made as well! But it's not one to take casually. It will require a step of faith built on a bedrock of solid facts—but faith just the same.

So whether you're a spiritual seeker looking for truth or a seasoned Christian looking for spiritual reinforcements, I trust you'll find helpful, life-giving answers in the pages ahead. And I hope you'll follow up this booklet by reading *The Case for Christ* book and seeing the movie, as well as delving into some of the great materials listed in the Recommended Resources.

Jesus promised in Matthew 7:7, "Seek and you will find." And as you do, I'll be praying for you and cheering you on from afar.

Lee Strobel

1

I have so many questions—and a few doubts—about the Christian faith. What should I do with them?

You are doing precisely what you need to do— you're being honest with yourself and open with your questions. That's the first step toward finding answers. If you do the opposite—bottling up your concerns in the hopes they'll go away— then they'll just fester and infect your entire spiritual life.

Instead, let me urge you to follow the wisdom of Scripture. Jesus said, "Everyone who asks receives; the one who seeks finds; and to the one who knocks, the door will be opened" (Matthew 7:8). This echoes a principle in the Old Testament: "You will seek me and find me when you seek me with all your heart" (Jeremiah 29:13).

I've struggled with spiritual questions for most of my life, and in some ways I still do. It's an ongoing process to find answers that satisfy my heart and soul. But even bouts of doubt can show we're thinking and growing, rather than simply clinging to what we've been told.

As I described in *The Case for Christ*, my greatest season of spiritual introspection came after my wife, Leslie, announced that she had become a Christian. That was hard news for a skeptical journalist to hear! But it set in motion my own journey of asking tough questions—and discovering unexpected answers. In the end, I concluded that it would take more faith for me to maintain my atheism than it would to become a Christian!

After almost two years of searching, I got on my knees and asked Jesus to forgive my sins and lead my life. It was a decision that changed everything; in fact, it was the pivotal moment of my life.

That decision, mixed with the research I did then and in the time since then, led me to a sense of confidence that there are satisfying answers to even our hardest questions. It's in that spirit that I write this book.

> Jesus stayed behind . . . sitting among the teachers, listening to them and asking them questions. Everyone who heard him was amazed at his understanding and his answers.
>
> LUKE 2:43, 46–47

2

Were there really ancient prophecies predicting details about the life and ministry of Jesus?

The Old Testament contains numerous predictions about the coming Messiah, and when you piece them all together, they create a "fingerprint" of who he would be and what he would do. The Bible teaches that we can have absolute confidence that whoever fits this fingerprint is truly the Messiah—and of all the people who ever walked the earth, only Jesus Christ matches it.

In *The Case for Christ*, I interviewed Louis Lapides, a Jewish man who encountered these prophecies years ago. "I was reading the Old Testament every day and seeing one prophecy after another," he said. "For instance, Deuteronomy talked about a prophet greater than Moses who will come and whom we should listen to. I thought, *Who can be greater than Moses?* It sounded like the Messiah—someone as great and respected as Moses but a greater teacher and a greater authority. I grabbed ahold of that and went searching for him."[1]

As Lapides progressed through the Scriptures, he was stopped cold by Isaiah 53. With clarity and specificity, in a haunting prediction wrapped in exquisite poetry, here was the picture of a Messiah who would suffer and die for the sins of Israel and the world—all written more than seven hundred years before Jesus walked the earth.

> He was despised and rejected by mankind,
>   a man of suffering, and familiar with pain.
> Like one from whom people hide their faces
>   he was despised, and we held him in low
>   esteem.
> Surely he took up our pain
>   and bore our suffering,
> yet we considered him punished by God,
>   stricken by him, and afflicted.
> But he was pierced for our transgressions,
>   he was crushed for our iniquities;
> the punishment that brought us peace was on
>   him,
>   and by his wounds we are healed.
> We all, like sheep, have gone astray,
>   each of us has turned to our own way;
> and the LORD has laid on him
>   the iniquity of us all. . . .
> For he bore the sin of many,
>   and made intercession for the transgressors.
>   ISAIAH 53:3–6, 12

Instantly Lapides recognized this as a portrait of Jesus of Nazareth! He began to understand the paintings he had seen as a child: the suffering Jesus, the crucified Jesus, the Jesus who had been "pierced for our transgressions" as he "bore the sin of many."

Over and over Lapides would come upon prophecies in the Old Testament—more than four dozen major predictions in all. Isaiah revealed the manner of the Messiah's birth (of a virgin, Isaiah 7:14); Micah pinpointed the place of his birth (Bethlehem, Micah 5:2); Genesis and Jeremiah specified his ancestry (a descendent of Abraham, Isaac, and Jacob, from the tribe of Judah, the house of David, Genesis 21:12; 49:8–12; Jeremiah 23:5–6); the Psalms foretold his betrayal, his accusation by false witnesses, his manner of death (pierced in the hands and feet, although crucifixion hadn't even been invented yet, Psalm 22); and his resurrection (he would not decay but would ascend on high, Psalm 16:10); and on and on. Each one chipped away at Lapides's skepticism about Jesus, until he was finally willing to take a drastic step.

One night in the Mojave Desert he cried out, "God, I've got to come to the end of this struggle. I have to know beyond a shadow of a doubt that

Jesus is the Messiah. I need to know that you, as the God of Israel, want me to believe this."[2]

God gave Lapides the certainty he was looking for, so he received the forgiveness and leadership of Christ and began following him from that time forward. Lapides later married Deborah, another Jewish follower of Jesus, and together they founded a fellowship of Jewish and Gentile believers where he served as the pastor for many years.

The Messianic prophecies played a huge role in leading Lapides to faith in Christ, and they were compelling to me when I encountered them as a skeptic—as they still are today.

> "This is what I told you while I was still with you: Everything must be fulfilled that is written about me in the Law of Moses, the Prophets and the Psalms."
>
> JESUS, AFTER HIS RESURRECTION,
> IN LUKE 24:44

3

Is there any historical evidence from outside the Bible to show it is true?

There are many outside sources that corroborate the claims of the Bible. Dr. Gary Habermas, in *The Historical Jesus*, details thirty-nine ancient sources documenting the life of Jesus, from which he enumerates more than one hundred reported facts concerning Jesus' life, teachings, crucifixion, and resurrection.[1]

What's more, twenty-four of the sources cited by Habermas, including seven secular sources and several of the earliest creeds of the church, specifically concern the divine nature of Jesus. "These creeds reveal that the church did not simply teach Jesus' deity a generation later . . . this doctrine is definitely present in the earliest church," said the historian.[2]

Professor Edwin Yamauchi adds, "When people begin religious movements, it's often not until many generations later that people record things about them, but the fact is that we have better historical documentation for Jesus than for the founder of any other ancient religion . . . [it's] quite impressive in terms of how much we can learn about him aside from the New Testament."³

I asked Dr. Yamauchi what we could conclude about Jesus from ancient non-Christian sources. "We would know that first, Jesus was a Jewish teacher; second, many people believed that he performed healings and exorcisms; third, some people believed he was the Messiah; fourth, he was rejected by the Jewish leaders; fifth, he was crucified under Pontius Pilate in the reign of Tiberius; sixth, despite this shameful death, his followers, who believed that he was still alive, spread beyond Palestine so that there were multitudes of them in Rome by AD 64; and seventh, all kinds of people from the cities and countryside—men and women, slave and free—worshiped him as God."⁴

This was indeed impressive outside corroboration for the claims of the New Testament—and more reasons we can have a confident faith in Christ.

> Jesus did many other things as well. If every one of them were written down, I suppose that even the whole world would not have room for the books that would be written.
>
> JOHN 21:25

4

With all the differences between
the New Testament manuscripts,
how can we trust the Bible?

This challenge has long been known but has
been amplified by agnostic professor Bart
Ehrman in his book *Misquoting Jesus*—which was
the top-selling religion book in America for many
weeks.

Ehrman points out that we don't have the
original copies of the New Testament.[1] That's
true—though we don't have the originals of any
ancient writings, sacred or secular. What we have
instead are handwritten copies.

Ehrman also states correctly that there are
between 200,000 and 400,000 variants, or differences, between the copies that we have.[2] So the
implication is clear: How can we trust the Bible
if it's pockmarked with errors? How do we really
know what the original documents said if we don't
actually possess any of them?

This has shaken the faith of some people—but
it need not. We have good reasons to believe the
New Testament has been reliably preserved for us.

First, the more copies you have of any document,

the more variations you'll have. So, for example, if you only have a handful of manuscript copies—as in the case of most ancient literature—then there won't be very many differences either. But when you have over 5,800 manuscript copies of the New Testament, then you'll also have many more variations between them. So the high number of variants is actually a by-product of the overwhelming quantity of copies that we have—and is a mark of strength.

Second, the more copies you have, the easier it is to determine what the original said, because there's so much more to compare between them in order to weed out mistakes.

I should add that up to 80 percent of the variants in the New Testament documents are minor spelling errors. And only 1 percent have some chance of affecting the meaning in some way. And even those are largely about insignificant issues—with not a single doctrine of the church in jeopardy.[3]

In the end, the New Testament has unprecedented support for its textual accuracy.

> "Blessed is the one who keeps the words of
> the prophecy written in this scroll."
> JESUS, IN REVELATION 22:7

5

Was Jesus really convinced he was the Son of God?

I asked that question of Dr. Ben Witherington III, the author of *The Christology of Jesus*, in our interview for *The Case for Christ*. Based on the evidence, Witherington replied:

> Did Jesus believe he was the Son of God, the anointed one of God? The answer is yes. Did he see himself as the Son of Man? The answer is yes. Did he see himself as the final Messiah? Yes, that's the way he viewed himself. Did he believe that anybody less than God could save the world? No, I don't believe he did.[1]

It's clear that Jesus' term for himself, "Son of God," points to his deity. This was confirmed in John 5:17 where he told the religious leaders who were challenging him, "My Father is always at his work to this very day, and I too am working." This claim infuriated these men, because they understood what he was really saying.

In fact, John—a disciple of Jesus—summarized the situation: "For this reason they tried all the more to kill him; not only was he breaking the Sabbath, but he was even calling God his own

Father, making himself equal with God" (John 5:18).

Jesus even went so far as to insist on belief in this claim—that he was the unique Son of God—as a litmus test for his followers. In Matthew 16:13–17, he asked his disciples who people thought he was. They replied, "Some say John the Baptist; others say Elijah; and still others, Jeremiah or one of the prophets."

"But what about you?" he asked. "Who do you say I am?"

Simon Peter answered, "You are the Messiah, the Son of the living God."

Jesus replied, "Blessed are you, Simon son of Jonah, for this was not revealed to you by flesh and blood, but by my Father in heaven."

Clearly Jesus knew he was the Son of God—and wanted us to know as well.

"For God so loved the world that he gave his one and only Son, that whoever believes in him shall not perish but have eternal life."

JESUS, IN JOHN 3:16

6

Jesus called himself the "Son of Man." Doesn't this mean he was merely human?

That's a natural way to see that phrase—in fact, it's what I thought when I first encountered it. But this illustrates why it's so important to study terms in their original language and context.

Scholars have shown that Jesus' repeated references to himself as the Son of Man were actually not a claim of humanity, though he certainly was human. Rather, the phrase came from an Old Testament passage, Daniel 7:13–14, in which the Son of Man has universal authority and everlasting dominion, and receives the worship of all nations. Theologian William Lane Craig summarized, "Thus, the claim to be the Son of Man would be in effect a claim to divinity."[1]

No one would have better understood what Jesus meant than the theologians of his day. So it's telling to see their reactions during his trial in Mark 14, where the high priest asked, "Are you the Messiah, the Son of the Blessed One?" (v. 61).

"I am," said Jesus. "And you will see the Son of Man sitting at the right hand of the Mighty One and coming on the clouds of heaven" (Mark

14:62). Jesus, in this one statement, affirmed that he was the Messiah, the Son of the Blessed One, the Son of Man, and he would one day come back.

That last part really grabbed their attention. If there was any doubt that his "Son of Man" reference alluded to the divine person described in Daniel, the "coming with the clouds of heaven," from Daniel 7:13, quickly removed it. This was a clear claim to deity!

Their reaction? "The high priest tore his clothes. 'Why do we need any more witnesses? . . . You have heard the blasphemy.'" Then it says, "They all condemned him as worthy of death" (Mark 14:63–64).

Their response confirmed what Jesus meant. He was the Son of Man, the incarnation of God, the Savior of the world.

> "For the Son of Man is going to come in his Father's glory with his angels, and then he will reward each person according to what they have done."
>
> JESUS, IN MATTHEW 16:27

Did Jesus' life demonstrate that
he was a divine person?

While Jesus made claims to divinity in a variety of ways, it's natural to ask whether his life backed up those claims. Here's a brief summary of some of the evidence.

Biblical theologians have long taught that the primary attributes of God are *omniscience* (all-knowing), *omnipresence* (present everywhere), *omnipotence* (all-powerful), *eternality* (always existed—and always will), and *immutability* (unchanging).

Every one of these attributes of God, says the New Testament, is found also in Jesus Christ:

- **Omniscience?** In John 16:30, the apostle John affirms of Jesus, "Now we can see that you know all things."
- **Omnipresence?** Jesus said in Matthew 28:20, "Surely I am with you always, to the very end of the age," and in Matthew 18:20, "Where two or three gather in my name, there am I with them."
- **Omnipotence?** "All authority in heaven and on earth has been given to me," Jesus said in Matthew 28:18.

- **Eternality?** John 1:1, 14 declares of Jesus, "In the beginning was the Word, and the Word was with God, and the Word was God. . . . The Word became flesh and made his dwelling among us."
- **Immutability?** Hebrews 13:8 says, "Jesus Christ is the same yesterday and today and forever."

Also, the Old Testament paints a portrait of God by using such descriptive titles as Alpha and Omega, Lord, Savior, King, Judge, Light, Rock, Redeemer, Shepherd, Creator, giver of life, forgiver of sin, and one who spoke with divine authority. It's fascinating to note that in the New Testament each and every one of those is also applied to Jesus.

The evidence for the deity of Christ is overwhelming. But there's one more attribute of God that really hits home for me because of how much I need it:

- God is also **omnibenevolent** (all-loving).

And Jesus said in John 15:13, "Greater love has no one than this: to lay down one's life for one's friends"—*and then he did it.*

"If you really know me, you will know my Father as well."

JESUS, IN JOHN 14:7

Jesus did many things, but what was his real mission?

Jesus—who was God incarnate—came for a very specific reason. He explained in Mark 10:45, "For even the Son of Man did not come to be served, but to serve, and *to give his life as a ransom for many*" (emphasis mine).

Why would Jesus talk in terms of making a payment to release captives? The answer is, *we're all captives to sin*. And because of our sin, we've incurred a debt we can't afford to pay. Romans 6:23 explains, "The wages of sin is death." This means we deserve a spiritual death penalty—one we'll have to pay for all eternity.

Thankfully, Jesus came to die on the cross to pay our ransom and set us free. He "suffered once for sins, the righteous for the unrighteous, to bring you to God" (1 Peter 3:18). This means Jesus paid the death penalty in our place. That's why Romans 6:23 ends with "but the gift of God is eternal life in Christ Jesus our Lord." No wonder the gospel is called *good news*!

But some people ask why God couldn't simply forgive people without sacrificing his Son. In response, philosopher Paul Copan, in our interview for *In Defense of Jesus* (formerly titled *The Case for the Real Jesus*), points to the parable in Matthew 18:21–35, which describes a king who forgives a great debt.

"Notice what happens in that parable. The king doesn't just forgive," Copan explains. "He also absorbs the debt. The king basically says he's going to bear the burden of the loss even though the servant owes him money. Similarly, Jesus paid the cost of our sin on the cross. It's like a child who breaks a neighbor's window. He may be too young to pay the price himself, so his parents pay it for him."[1]

We're like the servant—or the child. Thankfully God, in Christ, assumed and absorbed our debt. He paid our ransom in order to set captives like us—you and me—free for eternity.

Here is a trustworthy saying that deserves full acceptance: Christ Jesus came into the world to save sinners—of whom I am the worst.

1 TIMOTHY 1:15

The New Testament says Jesus sweat drops of blood when he was praying in the Garden of Gethsemane. Is that just a figure of speech?

That's what I thought when I was a skeptic. Then I started my research for *The Case for Christ*. I went to California to interview Dr. Alexander Metherell, a physician, research scientist, and expert on the crucifixion of Jesus.

"This is a known medical condition called *hematidrosis*. It's not very common, but it is associated with a high degree of psychological stress," he told me.

"What happens is that severe anxiety causes the release of chemicals that break down the capillaries in the sweat glands. As a result, there's a small amount of bleeding into these glands, and the sweat comes out tinged with blood. We're not talking about a lot of blood; it's just a very, very small amount."[1]

Interestingly, it was Luke, a physician, who noted this phenomenon. He said of Jesus in Luke 22:44: "And being in anguish, he prayed more earnestly, and his sweat was like drops of blood falling to the ground."

Jesus' anguish and passionate prayers over his impending torture and death could certainly have been enough to trigger this medical phenomenon. The *Journal of Medicine* analyzed seventy-six cases of hematidrosis and concluded that the most common causes were acute fear and intense mental contemplation.[2]

I asked Dr. Metherell what affect this bloody sweat would have had on Jesus. "What this did," he replied, "was set up the skin to be extremely fragile so that when Jesus was flogged by the Roman soldier the next day, his skin would have been very, very sensitive."

What could have prompted Jesus to willingly endure the misery of Gethsemane, the brutality of the flogging, and the unspeakable torment of the cross?

"Well," said Dr. Metherell, "I suppose the answer can be summed up in one word—and that would be *love*."

> But God demonstrates his own love for us in this: While we were still sinners, Christ died for us.
>
> ROMANS 5:8

10

A central claim of Christianity is that Jesus rose from the dead. Is there any solid evidence to support this?

The resurrection of Christ has been called the linchpin of the Christian faith. If Jesus really did rise from the dead, then this provides powerful evidence that his claims are true—including him being the Son of God, the prophesied Messiah, and the Savior of the World.

But if Jesus did not rise from the dead, then as the apostle Paul put it so bluntly, "your faith is futile; you are still in your sins" (1 Corinthians 15:17). In other words, *this is a really big deal*!

I reasoned as a skeptic that if I could refute the resurrection claims, I'd be off the hook with the God idea altogether. So I launched what turned out to be an almost two-year investigation of the historical evidence. What I discovered surprised me! There is a *wealth* of solid historical evidence that Jesus rose from the dead. Here's an overview, summed up in six terms that start with the letter *E*:

Execution

Perhaps, I thought, Jesus just passed out on the cross or faked his death. These were once popular theories among skeptics, but they've now been thoroughly discredited. In fact, even the atheist historian Gerd Lüdemann has acknowledged that the historical evidence for Jesus' execution is "indisputable."[1]

Empty Tomb

The New Testament reports that on the first Easter morning, the women found no body in the tomb. Peter and John later confirmed this for themselves. But to me the strongest evidence is that even the enemies of Jesus implicitly admitted that the tomb was empty. Rather than refute the claims that Jesus' burial place was vacant, they made up stories to explain *why* the body was missing (Matthew 28:11–15)—in effect, conceding that the tomb was unoccupied!

Eyewitnesses

Soon the disciples saw the risen Savior himself— some of them multiple times. Over forty days Jesus appeared to individuals and groups in a variety of circumstances. In all, we have nine ancient sources, inside and outside the New Testament, confirming the conviction of the disciples that they had encountered the risen Christ.[2]

Early Accounts

Multiple reports of Jesus' resurrection were circulating during the lifetimes of Jesus' contemporaries—people who would have been all too happy to point out the errors if the accounts had been invented. In fact, the earliest report of Jesus rising from the dead comes within *months* of his resurrection (recorded in 1 Corinthians 15:3–7)— far too quickly to have been a mere legend.

Extra-biblical Reports

Secular accounts confirm the contours of the New Testament. Historian Gary Habermas lists thirty-nine ancient sources *outside* the Bible that provide more than one hundred facts about Jesus' life, teachings, death, and resurrection.[3]

Emergence of the Church

Apart from the resurrection, it's hard to explain the beginnings of the church. Why? Because it emerged in the very city where Jesus had been crucified just a few weeks earlier—and it grew out of the claim that he had come back to life. If that claim were false, people would have laughed at the disciples. Instead, three thousand of them trusted in Christ and were baptized into the church (Acts 2:41).

I'll provide more details in the coming pages, but in the meantime I hope you can see why the case for the resurrection changed my mind—and eventually my heart and entire life.

> If Christ has not been raised, your faith is futile; you are still in your sins. Then those also who have fallen asleep in Christ are lost. If only for this life we have hope in Christ, we are of all people most to be pitied. But Christ has indeed been raised from the dead, the firstfruits of those who have fallen asleep.
>
> 1 CORINTHIANS 15:17–20

Some people claim Jesus' tomb was empty because someone stole his body. How do we know that's not what happened?

That same claim was made two thousand years ago. Matthew 28:12–13 reports that when Jesus' enemies heard his tomb was empty, they immediately "devised a plan." Specifically,

> They gave the soldiers a large sum of money, telling them, "You are to say, 'His disciples came during the night and stole him away while we were asleep.'"

Would you like to guess how many people this scheme fooled? Approximately *zero*! Why? Because it didn't even make sense. If the guards were sleeping, they wouldn't have *known* what happened to the body! And if they were awake, they certainly would not have let anybody steal it.

Furthermore, who would have had a motive to steal Jesus' body? Not the Jewish leaders; they wanted him dead in the first place. And certainly not the Romans; they wanted him to *stay* dead!

So that leaves us with only one other possible party: the disciples. But did they have the motive, the opportunity, or the wherewithal to take Jesus' body? Not at all! They were cowering in abject fear and regret over the death of their leader. All they wanted was to stay hidden in the shadows and out of trouble.

So to imagine that these dejected souls somehow concocted a plan to steal the body of the one who taught them never to steal, and then to tell lies about the one who taught them never to lie, all so they could be persecuted for the rest of their days while feigning a false hope over the return of their murdered Messiah . . . well, that stretches my mind beyond credulity.

For me—and I trust for you too—it's much easier to just accept the answer that the evidence supports: the tomb was empty because Jesus had risen.

> As they entered the tomb, they saw a young man dressed in a white robe sitting on the right side, and they were alarmed. "Don't be alarmed," he said. "You are looking for Jesus the Nazarene, who was crucified. He has risen! He is not here."
>
> MARK 16:5–6

Jesus appeared to his followers after his crucifixion—but how do we know they weren't just hallucinating?

That's a question I asked when I was first investigating the resurrection. People see all kinds of strange things—Jesus on burnt toast, the Virgin Mary's tears on paintings and statues, angels peering from the clouds. Why get worked up about a handful of zealots claiming to see a risen Jesus?

Then I actually studied the matter, and I found out there are good reasons to reject the hallucination hypothesis. Here are a few:

"The disciples were fearful, doubtful, and in despair after the crucifixion, whereas people who hallucinate need a fertile mind of expectancy or anticipation," Dr. Gary Habermas said to me. "Peter was hardheaded, for goodness' sake; James was a skeptic—certainly not good candidates for hallucinations.

"Also," Habermas continued, "hallucinations are comparably rare. They're usually caused by drugs or bodily deprivation. Yet we're supposed to believe that over a course of many weeks, people from all sorts of backgrounds, all kinds of temperaments, in various places, all experienced hallucinations?"[1]

In addition, psychologist Dr. Gary Collins explains, "Hallucinations are *individual* occurrences. By their very nature only one person can see a given hallucination at a time. They certainly aren't something which can be seen by a group of people."[2]

That made sense to me. If I asked you, "How did you like that dream I had last night?", you'd think I needed a bit more rest—or an appointment with Dr. Collins! Dreams, like hallucinations, are not shared events. Yet the earliest report we have about the resurrection says Jesus appeared to five hundred people at once! Besides, the disciples claimed they talked to and even ate with the risen Jesus (1 Corinthians 15:3–7, which will be discussed further in the next answer, and Luke 24:36–48).

When you look at all of the information, it becomes clear that the disciples and others actually encountered the resurrected Jesus.

> "Why are you troubled, and why do doubts rise in your minds? Look at my hands and my feet. It is I myself! Touch me and see; a ghost does not have flesh and bones, as you see I have."
>
> JESUS, IN LUKE 24:38–39

Weren't the reports of Jesus' death and resurrection written generations later—possibly distorting the story?

That used to be a popular claim. But we now know the entire New Testament, including the four gospels, was written within the time frame of the lives of Jesus' contemporaries—not generations later.[1] So there was simply not enough time for legend to replace the historical facts that were relayed by those early reporters.

But here's what's interesting: as early as the Gospels were, they were preceded by the even earlier writings of the apostle Paul. In one letter that Paul wrote within twenty-five years after the death of Christ, he includes a creed that had been formulated previously by the earliest Christians and then handed down to him:

> For what I received I passed on to you as of first importance: that Christ died for our sins according to the Scriptures, that he was buried, that he was raised on the third day according to the Scriptures, and that he appeared to Cephas, and then to the Twelve. After that, he appeared to more than five hundred of the

brothers and sisters at the same time, most of whom are still living, though some have fallen asleep. Then he appeared to James, then to all the apostles. (1 Corinthians 15:3–7)

"Many scholars believe Paul received this creed from Peter and James while visiting with them in Jerusalem three years after his conversion," said New Testament scholar Michael Licona. "That would be within five years of the crucifixion. Think about that—it's really amazing! . . . Not only is it extremely early, but it was apparently given to Paul by eyewitnesses or others he deemed reliable, which heightens its credibility even more."[2]

Since the beliefs that make up that early creed go back even further in time, this means we have a report of the resurrection that goes back virtually to the cross itself. Said historian James D. G. Dunn: "This tradition, we can be entirely confident, was formulated as tradition within months of Jesus' death."[3]

Put another way, *we have a news flash from the ancient world*!

> For we did not follow cleverly devised stories when we told you about the coming of our Lord Jesus Christ in power, but we were eyewitnesses of his majesty.
>
> 2 PETER 1:16

14

What difference does it make today that a man rose from the dead two thousand years ago?

I once wondered the same thing—but soon realized the implications of Jesus' resurrection were huge. Here are three examples:

The resurrection establishes Jesus' identity.

After being asked by the Pharisees for some kind of proof that he was who he claimed to be, Jesus said in Matthew 12:39–40, "A wicked and adulterous generation asks for a sign! But none will be given it except the sign of the prophet Jonah. For as Jonah was three days and three nights in the belly of a huge fish, so the Son of Man will be three days and three nights in the heart of the earth." Jesus made it clear that the ultimate validation of his claims would be his own death, burial, and resurrection. These would show that he truly was the Son of God.

The resurrection validates the Christian faith.

This point flows from the last one. As the unique Son of God, Jesus is "calling God his own Father, making himself equal with God" (John 5:18). This

validates the Christian doctrine of the Trinity—
one God in three persons—Father, Son, and Holy
Spirit. And because Jesus is God, he is also Lord,
so we need to believe and obey him (Luke 6:46;
Matthew 28:20).

The resurrection energizes the gospel message.

Jesus came "to give his life as a ransom for many"
(Matthew 20:28). Paul explains this further: "He
was delivered over to death for our sins and was
raised to life for our justification" (Romans 4:25).
Both elements are key to the gospel: Jesus' *death*
made the necessary payment; Jesus' *resurrection*
enabled him to apply that payment and to give us
life. He has provided everything. All we need to
do is say yes and to follow him as our forgiver and
leader.

> But Christ has indeed been raised from the
> dead, the firstfruits of those who have fallen
> asleep. For since death came through a man,
> the resurrection of the dead comes also
> through a man. For as in Adam all die, so in
> Christ all will be made alive.
>
> 1 CORINTHIANS 15:20–22

15 ·····································

How can belief in the resurrection of Christ impact someone personally?

I posed that question to Dr. Gary Habermas, one of the world's leading resurrection scholars. His answer harkened back to an earlier time in his life, when his wife, Debbie, was slowly dying of stomach cancer. Caught off guard by the tenderness of the moment, all I could do was listen.

"I sat on our porch," he began. "My wife was upstairs dying. Except for a few weeks, she was home through it all. It was the worst thing that could possibly happen.

"But do you know what was amazing? My students would call me and say, 'At a time like this, aren't you glad about the resurrection?' As sober as those circumstances were, I had to smile for two reasons. First, my students were trying to cheer me up with my own teaching. And second, it worked.

"I knew if God were to come to me, I'd ask only one question: 'Lord, why is Debbie up there in bed?' And I think God would respond by asking gently, 'Gary, did I raise my Son from the dead?'

"I'd say, 'Come on, Lord, I've written seven

books on that topic! Of course he was raised from the dead. But I want to know about Debbie!'

"I think he'd keep coming back to the same question—'Did I raise my Son from the dead?' 'Did I raise my Son from the dead?'—until I got his point: the resurrection says that if Jesus was raised two thousand years ago, there's an answer to Debbie's death in 1995. And do you know what? It worked for me while I was sitting on the porch, and it still works today."

Habermas locked eyes with mine. "That's not some sermon," he said quietly. "I believe that with all my heart. If there's a resurrection, there's a heaven. If Jesus was raised, Debbie was raised. And I will be someday too.

"Then I'll see them both."[1]

And if the Spirit of him who raised Jesus from the dead is living in you, he who raised Christ from the dead will also give life to your mortal bodies because of his Spirit who lives in you.

ROMANS 8:11

16

Isn't it narrow-minded to claim that Jesus is the only pathway to God?

It certainly would be narrow-minded if Christians were saying, "Jesus is the only way because he's *my* way," or if they were just trying to edge out the competition from other religions. But this idea did not originate with some pastor or theologian. It goes back to Jesus himself. He's the one who said, "I am the way and the truth and the life. No one comes to the Father except through me" (John 14:6).

People who bristle at this idea are ultimately arguing with Jesus—not with the Christians who are simply trying to be faithful to his teachings.

But was *Jesus* narrow-minded? Well, in a sense he was. In fact, in the Sermon on the Mount he said, "Enter through the narrow gate. For wide is the gate and broad is the road that leads to destruction, and many enter through it. But small is the gate and narrow the road that leads to life, and only a few find it" (Matthew 7:13–14).

If Jesus was right about this, then he was being appropriately narrow-minded. He was being like parents who are narrow enough to insist that their children walk on the sidewalk and not in the street, or a doctor who limits his prescriptions to medicine that will actually help people rather than poison them, or the airline pilot who restricts his landing options to that narrow path to life called a runway, rather than trying to put the airplane down on a cornfield or a beach.

You see, we really *want* narrow approaches—as long as they are based on truth and point us in the direction that's best for us.

Jesus gave us every reason to believe he was telling the truth and that he loves us enough to lead us toward forgiveness, life, and an eternity with him.

> "I am the gate; whoever enters through me will be saved. They will come in and go out, and find pasture. The thief comes only to steal and kill and destroy; I have come that they may have life, and have it to the full."
>
> JESUS, IN JOHN 10:9–10

17

There are so many other religions out there. How can we be sure that Christianity is the right one?

No doubt about it—people believe all kinds of religious ideas, and most people are sincere in their beliefs. We should treat them with gentleness and respect (1 Peter 3:15) and do all we can to protect their rights—as well as our own—to practice religion freely.

I also know that *people can be sincere but sincerely wrong*. In fact it's impossible that all the religions could be right, since they contradict each other on so many fundamental points. For example, look at what these religions teach about God:

- Buddhism historically denies that God exists (*atheism*).
- Hinduism teaches that everything is part of an all-pervasive, impersonal god (*pantheism*).
- Christianity teaches that there is one God who is personal and who created everything (*theism*).

As one person put it, if all these religions are true, then God must be schizophrenic—because he doesn't even know who he is, but tells one group one thing about himself while telling others something completely different!

Well, God is not schizophrenic—so we're forced to choose between belief systems. How should we do this? Should we base our decision on our traditions, or on what some authority figure tells us to believe, or perhaps on what we feel in our hearts? Those are dangerous ways to decide.

My contention, and the approach I've used throughout my writings, is that we should choose our beliefs based on where logic and the evidence point (while asking God for guidance). And it's with that approach that I've concluded Christianity—over any other worldview—squares with the facts of science, philosophy, and history.

More than that, my own experience has borne this out. Psalm 34:8 invites us, "Taste and see that the LORD is good; blessed is the one who takes refuge in him." Well, as one who has been tasting and seeing for more than three decades—and experiencing those blessings—I can testify that the psalmist was right: the Lord is real, and he is good.

> "I am the LORD your God,
>   who teaches you what is best for you,
>   who directs you in the way you should go."
>   ISAIAH 48:17

You've said you came to realize you didn't have enough faith to maintain your atheism. Can you explain what you mean?

There's a lot of confusion about *faith*. Some believe faith actually contradicts facts. "The whole point of faith," scoffed Michael Shermer of *The Skeptical Inquirer*, "is to believe regardless of the evidence, which is the very antithesis of science."[1]

That's not my understanding. I see faith as *a reasonable step in the same direction that the evidence is pointing*. It's doing what I did as a journalist—following the facts wherever they lead and then making a sound conclusion based on the weight of the information, even though I couldn't prove something 100 percent.

Given that definition, it's easy to see that every point of view, religious or secular, involves a measure of faith. As an atheist, for example, I concluded that there was no God based on what I thought to be good reasons, even though I couldn't prove he didn't exist. That was faith.

But when I started investigating Christianity, I began finding more and more evidence pointing away from atheism and toward belief in God. As I looked into science, for example, I realized I'd previously accepted, largely by faith, these misguided ideas:

- Nothing produces everything.
- Non-life produces life.
- Randomness produces finely tuned design.
- Chaos produces information.
- Unconsciousness produces consciousness.
- Non-reason produces reason.

In addition, I discovered that the historical evidence establishes the reliability of the New Testament, demonstrates the fulfillment of ancient prophecies in the life of Jesus, and supports the reality of Jesus' resurrection—authenticating his claim to being the unique Son of God.

The range, variety, depth, and breathtaking persuasive power of the evidence, from both science and history, affirmed the credibility of Christianity to the degree that my doubts simply washed away.

In the end, putting my trust in the God of the Bible was nothing less than the most rational decision I could make. I merely permitted the torrent of facts to carry me along to their most logical conclusion: *faith in Christ makes sense like nothing else.*

> Now faith is confidence in what we hope for
> and assurance about what we do not see.
>
> HEBREWS 11:1

Now that we've explored a lot of questions and answers, what should I do with the information?

If you're already a follower of Christ, then I trust that for you, as for me, the rigors of intellectual scrutiny have helped your faith emerge deeper, richer, more resilient, and more certain than ever. I hope this culminates in your having a truly confident faith—and that it emboldens you to share that faith with others.

If you're not yet a Christian, I trust that by reading answer after answer in this booklet, you're discovering, as I did, that the case for Christ is powerful and persuasive. If so, all that's left now is to talk to God and tell him you're ready to turn from your sins and receive his grace through Christ. Then you'll become his son or daughter, embarking on a spiritual adventure that will last throughout your lifetime—and into eternity.

But maybe important questions still linger. Perhaps I didn't address the objection that's uppermost in your mind. If so, I hope the information in these pages will at least encourage you to continue your investigation. I'd also like to echo the advice I gave at the beginning of the book:

1. Keep pursuing your search as a front-burner issue.

C. S. Lewis said that "Christianity is . . . if true, of infinite importance."[1] Knowing that, keep seeking answers diligently.

2. Keep your mind open and continue to follow the evidence.

I hope that *The Case for Christ* book and movie, as well as some of my other *Case* books, will help with that process, along with what's been written by the many experts I've quoted throughout these answers. And be sure to study the Bible as well.

3. When the evidence is in, reach a verdict.

Resolve that once you've gathered a sufficient amount of information, you'll make a decision, knowing you'll never have full resolution of every single issue. You may even want to whisper a prayer in the meantime, asking God to guide you to the truth about him.

And through it all, you'll have my sincere encouragement as you continue taking steps toward Christ.

> "You will seek me and find me when you seek me with all your heart."
>
> JEREMIAH 29:13

**Honestly, this is all starting to make sense.
But how can I know for sure that my sins
are forgiven and I'm part of God's family?**

I remember pondering that question at the end
of my spiritual investigation. I reached the place
where I knew the weight of the evidence pointed to
a risen Savior, and then I asked myself, *Is that it?
Do I just acknowledge this truth and keep on living
my life as I did before starting this journey?*

But then, as you may have seen in *The Case
for Christ* book or movie, I grappled with a verse
in the Bible, John 1:12, which says, "As many as
received Him, to them He gave the right to become
children of God, even to those who believe in His
name" (NASB). This verse has three parts, which
can be put into a simple formula:

Believe + Receive = Become

I realized I had already fulfilled the first part.
Based on the historical data, I'd come to *believe*
that Jesus is the Son of God who proved it by rising
from the dead. But this was not enough. The verse
said I also needed to *receive* the gift of forgiveness

and eternal life that Jesus purchased for me on the cross.

So I got down on my knees and admitted to God my lifetime of sin, and I told him I wanted—right then and there—to receive Jesus as my forgiver and leader. Do you know what happened? By the time I ended that prayer, I knew I had *become* a child of God, just as the verse promised.

Then, over time, my philosophy, worldview, attitude, values, character, and motives began to change—all for the better. And yours can too!

All you need to do is *believe* that Jesus is the Son of God as he claimed to be, that he died to pay for your sins, and that he rose to give you life. Then pray to *receive* him as your forgiver and leader—which you can do right now—and you will immediately *become* a child of the heavenly Father.

I can't encourage you more strongly to take that step. You'll be glad you did—not just for today, but for all of eternity.

> If you declare with your mouth, "Jesus is Lord," and believe in your heart that God raised him from the dead, you will be saved. For it is with your heart that you believe and are justified, and it is with your mouth that you profess your faith and are saved.
>
> ROMANS 10:9–10

Notes

Chapter 2

1. Lee Strobel, *The Case for Christ* (Grand Rapids, MI: Zondervan, 1998), 177.
2. Ibid., 179–80.

Chapter 3

1. Gary Habermas, *The Historical Jesus* (Nashville: Thomas Nelson, 1988).
2. Strobel, *The Case for Christ*, 91.
3. Ibid., 86–87.
4. Ibid., 87.

Chapter 4

1. Bart D. Ehrman, *Misquoting Jesus* (San Francisco: HarperSanFrancisco, 2005), 7.
2. Ibid., 89–90.
3. See discussion with Daniel Wallace in "Challenge #2" in Lee Strobel, *In Defense of Jesus* (formerly titled *The Case for the Real Jesus*) (Grand Rapids, MI: Zondervan, 2007), especially 85–87.

Chapter 5

1. Strobel, *The Case for Christ*, 140–41.

Chapter 6

1. William Lane Craig, *The Son Rises* (Chicago: Moody Press, 1981), 140.

Chapter 8

1. Strobel, *In Defense of Jesus*, 255.

Chapter 9

1. My full interview with Dr. Alexander Metherell is in chapter 11 of Strobel, *The Case for Christ*, 191ff.
2. J. E. Holoubek and A. E. Holoubek, "Blood, Sweat and Fear: 'A Classification of Hematidrosis,'" *Journal of Medicine* 1996, 27 (3–4): 115–33, http://www.ncbi.nlm.nih.gov/pubmed/8982961.

Chapter 10

1. Gerd Lüdemann, *The Resurrection of Christ: A Historical Inquiry* (Amherst, NY: Prometheus Books, 2004), 50.
2. Strobel, *The Case for Christ*, 90–91.
3. Habermas, *The Historical Jesus*.

Chapter 12

1. Strobel, *The Case for Christ*, 239.
2. Ibid., 238–39.

Chapter 13

1. F. F. Bruce, *The New Testament Documents: Are They Reliable?* (Grand Rapids, MI: Eerdmans, 1978), 12.
2. Strobel, *In Defense of Jesus*, 115.
3. James D. G. Dunn, *Jesus Remembered* (Grand Rapids, MI: Eerdmans, 2003), 855.

Chapter 15

1. Strobel, *The Case for Christ*, 241–42.

Chapter 18

1. Michael Shermer, *How We Believe* (New York: W. H. Freeman, 2000), 123.

Chapter 19

1. C. S. Lewis, *God in the Dock* (Copyright 1970, By the Trustees of the Estate of C. S. Lewis; Grand Rapids, MI: Eerdmans, reprinted in 2001), 101.

Recommended Resources

Lee Strobel, *The Case for Christ, Updated and Expanded Edition* (Zondervan, 1998, 2016).

Lee Strobel, *The Case for Faith* (Zondervan, 2000).

Lee Strobel, *The Case for a Creator* (Zondervan, 2004).

Lee Strobel, *In Defense of Jesus,* formerly *The Case for the Real Jesus* (Zondervan, 2007, 2016).

Note: Student and Kids editions of these *Case* books also available

Lee Strobel, *The Case for Grace* (Zondervan, 2014).

Lee Strobel, *The Case for Hope* (Zondervan, 2015).

Lee Strobel, *The Case for Christ Study Bible* (Zondervan, 2010).

Lee Strobel, *The Case for Christianity Answer Book* (Zondervan, 2014).

Lee Strobel and Mark Mittelberg, *Today's Moment of Truth* (Zondervan, 2016).

Mark Mittelberg, *Confident Faith: Building a Firm Foundation for Your Beliefs* (Tyndale, 2013).

Mark Mittelberg, *The Questions Christians Hope No One Will Ask (With Answers)* (Tyndale, 2010).

Mark Mittelberg, *The Reason Why: Faith Makes Sense* (Tyndale, 2011).

William Lane Craig, *On Guard: Defending Your Faith with Reason and Precision* (David C. Cook, 2010).

William Lane Craig, *Reasonable Faith* (Crossway, 2008).

Josh and Sean McDowell, *More Than a Carpenter* (Tyndale, 2009).

J. Warner Wallace, *Cold-Case Christianity* (David C. Cook, 2013).

Gary R. Habermas and Michael R. Licona, *The Case for the Resurrection of Jesus* (Kregel, 2004).

Norman L. Geisler and Frank Turek, *I Don't Have Enough Faith to Be an Atheist* (Crossway, 2004).

C. S. Lewis, *Mere Christianity* (Macmillan, 1952).

Meet Lee Strobel

The story of Lee Strobel's journey from atheism to Christianity is portrayed in the motion picture *The Case for Christ*, based on his bestselling book by that title. He is the former legal editor of the *Chicago Tribune* and now serves as Professor of Christian Thought at Houston Baptist University.

Described in the *Washington Post* as "one of the evangelical community's most popular apologists," Lee has written more than twenty books, including the award-winning *The Case for Faith*, *The Case for a Creator*, and *The Case for Grace*. Lee and his wife, Leslie, live in Texas, where he is a Teaching Pastor at Woodlands Church.

IF YOU LIKED READING THIS BOOK, YOU MAY ENJOY THESE OTHER TITLES FROM

Lee Strobel

ISBN: 9780310350576

THE CASE FOR CHRIST A seasoned journalist chases down the biggest story in history in *The Case for Christ*. Retracing his own spiritual journey from atheism to faith, former *Chicago Tribune* legal editor Lee Strobel cross-examines a dozen experts with tough, point-blank questions in search of credible evidence that Jesus of Nazareth was positively the Son of God. This riveting quest for the truth about history's most compelling figure reads like a captivating, fast-paced novel, yet it's anything *but* fiction!

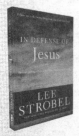

ISBN: 9780310344681

IN DEFENSE OF JESUS Former award-winning legal editor Lee Strobel explores such hot-button questions as:

- Did the church suppress ancient non-biblical documents that paint a more accurate picture of Jesus than the four Gospels?
- Did the church distort the truth about Jesus by tampering with early New Testament texts?
- Did Christianity steal its core ideas from early mythology?

Evaluate the arguments and evidence being advanced by prominent atheists, liberal theologians, Muslim scholars, and others. Sift through expert testimony. Reach your own verdict with *In Defense of Jesus*.